# —The Essential—
# ITALIAN
# COOKBOOK

# The Essential
# ITALIAN
# COOKBOOK

## 50 CLASSIC RECIPES,
## WITH STEP-BY-STEP PHOTOGRAPHS

EDITED BY

HEATHER THOMAS

COURAGE BOOKS

AN IMPRINT OF RUNNING PRESS
PHILADELPHIA • LONDON

This edition first published in the United States in 1995
by Courage Books, an imprint of Running Press Book Publishers.

9 8 7 6 5 4 3 2 1
Digit on the right indicates the number of this printing.

Library of Congress Cataloging-in-Publication Number 94-80087

ISBN 1-56138-598-0

Designed and produced by SP Creative Design
Editor and writer: Heather Thomas
Art director: Al Rockall
Designer: Rolando Ugolini
Special photography: Graham Kirk
Step-by-step photography: GGS Photographics, Norwich
Food preparation: Maxine Clark and Dawn Stock
Food styling for cover photograph: Gillian MacLaurin
Styling: Helen Payne
Produced by Mandarin Offset
Printed and bound in Hong Kong

Published by Courage Books, an imprint of
Running Press Book Publishers
125 South Twenty-second Street
Philadelphia, PA 19103-4399

**Notes**

**1.** Standard spoon measurements are used in all recipes.
1 tablespoon = one 15 ml spoon
1 teaspoon = one 5 ml spoon

**2.** Eggs should be medium unless otherwise stated.

**3.** Milk should be whole unless otherwise stated.

**4.** Fresh herbs should be used unless otherwise stated. If
unavailable, use dried herbs as an alternative.
1 tablespoon fresh herbs = 1 teaspoon dried herbs

**5.** Ovens should be preheated to the specified temperature. If
using a convection oven, follow the manufacturer's instructions
for adjusting the time and temperature.

# CONTENTS

# INTRODUCTION

Italian cooking is incredibly diverse and has evolved over many centuries. It derives from many classic European traditions: Roman, Byzantine and Greek. However, Italian food, as we know it today, stems from the Renaissance and the new discoveries and developments in the arts and sciences. Throughout northern and central Italy, in Florence, Venice, Milan and Rome, there was a new interest in food and a flowering of cooking skills as the great rulers experimented with new ingredients from the Far East and the New World.

The classic recipes from this exciting period of Italian history have been passed down through the generations and are now an established part of family and regional cooking. Every region has its own specialties, which are characterized by its climate, geography and local produce and fresh ingredients. Rome sits on the dividing line between the robust tomato and garlic flavored peasant dishes of the Mediterranean south, and the more sophisticated and elegant dishes of the north.

Effectively, there is no real "Italian" food, but there are classic Venetian, Roman, Sicilian, Bolognese and Neapolitan dishes, for example. From northern Italy come nourishing bean and vegetable soups, rustic stews, pasta in creamy sauces and delicate veal dishes, whereas from the south there are charcoal-grilled fish with vivid tomato sauces, caramelized oranges, sweet ricotta and mascarpone flans studded with crystallized fruit, and colorful stews of sweet peppers, eggplants, tomatoes and olives which grow in the warm southern sun.

In Italy, good food and wine are a way of life, an intrinsic part of the Italian character and culture. Italians cook with the freshest ingredients of the highest quality: fine regional cheeses, local sausages, tender beef and veal, country hams, fresh fish and seafood, free-range chickens and numerous varieties of fresh pasta.

Family meals are rituals and consist of several courses. They start with *antipasti* – such as stuffed vegetables, prosciutto, salami or seafood salad – followed by *minestra* (soup), and then pasta or a risotto, a fish or meat course with vegetables or salad, and then dessert and cheeses.

## Anchovies

Packed in oil or salty brine, anchovies are a characteristic ingredient in many classic recipes from Piedmont and the south (Sicily and Calabria), especially bean dishes and stews. They are essential for making *bagna cauda,* a garlic and anchovy-flavored dip from Piedmont, which is served with raw vegetable *crudités*.

## Arugola (rocket)

These dark green leaves have a distinctive peppery flavor and are often added to salads. They can be bought in many supermarkets, or you can grow them yourself.

## Basil

This pungent, aromatic herb is used widely throughout Italy to flavor tomato sauces, salads, stews and casseroles. It is the essential ingredient in pesto, a sauce made from pounding garlic, pine nuts, olive oil, Parmesan cheese and fresh basil leaves, and which is served with gnocchi or fresh pasta. Fresh basil is always preferable to dried, and can be purchased in many supermarkets either in packets or growing in small pots all the year round.

## Beans (fagioli)

Dried speckled borlotti beans or white cannellini beans are the beans most often used in soups and salads. They must be soaked in water overnight and then rinsed and drained before using. To cook them, bring to the boil in fresh water and then boil vigorously for a few minutes before reducing the heat to a simmer. Cook for about 1 hour, or until tender. Do not add salt to the cooking water as it will harden the beans.

## Ceps (porcini)

These mushrooms are highly prized and quite expensive. Fresh ceps are hard to find but you can use the dried ones, which are available from most good Italian delicatessens and have a rich, concentrated flavor. Soak them first in warm water for 20-30 minutes.

## Mozzarella

This fresh cheese is traditionally made from buffalo's milk and is sold packaged in its own whey. It should be dripping fresh with an elastic texture. It is the classic topping for pizza.

## Olive oil

You can choose between fruity green oils, which make wonderful salad dressings, and lighter golden ones, which are used for frying and tossing pasta. Really, there is no substitute for olive oil in Italian cooking, and sunflower or vegetable oils are not suitable – they do not have the same flavor. In the north, butter is used in many dishes instead of oil.

It is worth investing in good olive oil, even if it is a little more expensive than the cheaper brands. Extra virgin oil, made from the first cold pressing of the olives, is best for dressing salads. Virgin olive oil is more suitable for cooked dishes and sauces.

## Pancetta

This is raw pork belly which has been cured in salt and spices. It is usually used as a basis for stews and sauces, diced and then fried in olive oil with onion and garlic. If you cannot obtain pancetta, you can substitute ham or bacon instead.

## Parmesan

One of Italy's oldest and best-known cheeses, Parmesan is extremely hard and is aged over a long period, sometimes several years. It is sold split into rough lumps or ready-grated. To appreciate its strong flavor, it is best to buy it in pieces and then grate it freshly over pasta dishes.

## Pasta

There are scores of different types of pasta, and every region has its own particular specialties and ways of serving them. You can make it yourself, or buy it freshly made or dried, colored pink with tomato paste, green with spinach or even black with cuttlefish ink. Pasta is really only flour and water, sometimes enriched with an egg, but it is one of the most versatile Italian foods and may be baked, stuffed, tossed in sauces or vinaigrette dressing. It is found everywhere, all over Italy, in a variety of shapes and sizes (cylinders, spirals, shells, tubes, sheets and bows) and rejoices in wonderful evocative names – tortellini, ravioli, spaghetti, pappardelle, cappellacci, fettuccine and tagliatelle, to name but a few.

Pasta should be cooked uncovered in plenty of boiling water, to which a little oil and a generous pinch of salt have been added, until it is tender but still firm to the bite (*al dente*). Drain quickly and add a little butter or oil before using.

## Pine nuts (pignoli)

These small creamy nuts are gathered from the cones of the stone or umbrella pine. They add texture and a distinctive aromatic flavor to many savory dishes as well as cakes and biscuits. They are also an essential ingredient in pesto sauce.

## Polenta

This yellow maize flour hails from northern Italy and is particularly popular in Lombardy and the Veneto region around Venice. It is boiled and then served steaming hot with stews, or it can be left to cool and solidify and may then be cut into slices and broiled, baked or fried in olive oil. Unfortunately, polenta is time consuming to cook and needs continuous stirring to get a smooth, lump-free finish. However, you can now buy quicker-cooking versions which take the hard work out of preparing polenta.

## Prosciutto crudo

The best known of these cured raw hams are Parma and San Daniele, which are sold cut into wafer-thin slices. Prosciutto is salted and air-dried and usually has a faintly sweet flavor. It is often served as an *antipasto* dish with fresh figs or melon, or may be used in stuffings for veal and chicken.

## Rice

The most commonly used rice is the short-grained Arborio variety. This has been grown in Lombardy for over 600 years and is an essential ingredient in risottos – the classic rice dishes of northern Italy. The grains swell to two or three times their original size and are plump and round. They have a moist, creamy consistency and are slightly firm when cooked. The secret of a good risotto is to cook it very slowly over low heat until all of the liquid has been absorbed and the rice is tender.

## Salami

There are many regional varieties of salami, some of which are flavored with peppercorns, garlic, herbs or chiles. They are usually made from ground pork and are flecked liberally with white fat. Salami is usually served thinly sliced, often with olives, as an *antipasto* dish, or may be added to stews and soups. Mortadella from Bologna is one of the largest and best known of these preserved sausages. The Napoli salami is hot and spicy, whereas the Milano is milder with a fine texture.

## Tomatoes

These are essential to many Italian dishes, especially in the south. The Italian word for tomato is *pomodoro*, or "golden apple." Tomatoes are used fresh, canned, puréed, concentrated, sieved, sun-dried or preserved in fruity olive oil. Plum tomatoes are most commonly used for making sauces, which are flavored with onion and garlic and served with pasta, vegetables, meat and fish dishes.

## Equipment and utensils

Most Italian cooking utensils and kitchen gadgets are standard items in the western world, but there are a few specialist items that you might consider buying.

**Coffee maker:** you can buy genuine Italian machines for making expresso and cappuccino coffee. These range from the humble and inexpensive Moka-express and Neapolitan coffee maker to expensive steel and chrome hissing machines.

**Pasta machine:** this is very useful for making home-made pasta and reduces the time and labor of making it by hand. You can buy manual or electric machines but they are not worth the investment unless you adore pasta and plan to make it regularly.

**Pasta wheel:** this is a useful little gadget in wood or metal for cutting ravioli.

**Pestle and mortar:** in Italy, these are often made of marble. They are useful for making pesto sauce and pounding herbs and spices.

# PASTA CON I FAGIOLI

*White bean and noodle soup*

**1** Drain the beans and put in a large saucepan with the pork, onion, carrot, celery, garlic, parsley, sage, bay leaf and enough water to cover. Bring to the boil, then reduce the heat, cover the pan and simmer gently for 2 hours, or until the beans are soft.

**2** Put one cupful of beans through a food mill or rub through a sieve. Stir the puréed beans back into the soup. Season to taste with salt and pepper and bring back to the boil.

PREPARATION: SOAKING
OVERNIGHT
COOKING: 2½ HOURS
SERVES: 4-6

**3** Add the spaghetti or noodles to the soup, and boil for about 12 minutes, or until the pasta is cooked and tender but still firm to the bite (*al dente*).

| 1¼ cups dried white beans, soaked overnight |
| --- |
| ½ pound pork belly with skin |
| 1 onion, finely chopped |
| 1 carrot, finely chopped |
| 1 celery stick, finely chopped |
| 1 garlic clove, minced |
| 3 parsley sprigs, finely chopped |
| 1 sprig of sage, chopped |
| 1 bay leaf |
| salt and freshly ground black pepper |
| 6 ounces spaghetti, ribbon noodles or vermicelli |
| 2 tablespoons olive oil |

**4** Remove the pork from the soup. Cut off the rind and cut the meat into small pieces. Just before serving, drizzle the olive oil into the soup, and stir in the pork and a generous grinding of black pepper. Transfer to a tureen or individual serving dishes.

# MINESTRONE

*Italian vegetable soup*

1 Place the navy beans in a large bowl and cover with water. Leave to soak for 8 hours or overnight. Drain the beans and then rinse under running cold water.

2 Heat the oil in a large saucepan and add the onions, garlic and bacon. Sauté gently for about 5 minutes, stirring occasionally, until soft and golden brown.

3 Add the beans, water, herbs and tomatoes, cover the pan and simmer gently for 2 hours. Add the carrots and simmer for 10 minutes. Stir in the potatoes and turnip and cook for another 10 minutes.

| |
|---|
| ½ cup navy beans |
| 3 tablespoons oil |
| 2 onions, chopped |
| 2 garlic cloves, minced |
| 2-3 rindless bacon slices, chopped |
| 7½ cups water |
| 1 teaspoon chopped fresh marjoram |
| ½ teaspoon chopped fresh thyme |
| 4 tomatoes, skinned, seeded and chopped |
| 2 carrots, diced |
| 2 potatoes, diced |
| 1 small turnip, diced |
| 1-2 celery sticks |
| ½ pound cabbage |
| ½ cup small pasta shapes |
| 1 tablespoon chopped fresh parsley |
| salt and freshly ground black pepper |
| 3 tablespoons grated Parmesan cheese + extra to serve |

PREPARATION: 20 MINUTES +
SOAKING OVERNIGHT
COOKING: 2½ HOURS
SERVES: 6

4 Chop the celery and shred the cabbage. Add to the soup with the pasta shapes and cook for 10 minutes, or until the pasta and all the vegetables are tender. Add the parsley and seasoning to taste. Stir in the Parmesan and then ladle into individual soup bowls. Serve immediately with extra Parmesan cheese.

# INSALATA DI MARE

*Seafood salad*

1 | Soak the mussels in a bowl of cold water and discard any that are open or rise to the surface. Scrub them well to remove any barnacles, and then remove the beards.

3 | Place the scallops, angler fish and squid on a piece of foil. Sprinkle with the juice of ½ lemon, dot with butter and scatter 1 tablespoon of the parsley over the top. Fold the foil over to form a "parcel," seal the edges and cook in a preheated oven at 375° for 20 minutes, or until cooked.

2 | Put the mussels in a deep saucepan and add the water. Cover with a lid and steam over high heat, shaking the pan occasionally, until the mussels open. Steam for 2 more minutes and then drain and set aside to cool. Discard any that do not open and remove the others from their shells.

PREPARATION: 25 MINUTES
COOKING: 20 MINUTES
SERVES: 4-6

| |
|---|
| 1 pound fresh mussels in their shells |
| ½ cup water |
| 8 shucked scallops, cut into pieces |
| ¾ pound angler fish, cubed |
| ¼ pound squid, sliced |
| juice of 2 lemons |
| 1 tablespoon butter |
| 3 tablespoons finely chopped fresh parsley |
| 12 jumbo shrimp |
| 2 garlic cloves, minced |
| 4 tablespoons olive oil |
| salt and freshly ground black pepper |

4 | Put the shrimp in a baking dish and sprinkle with garlic, the juice of ½ lemon and 1 tablespoon of the chopped parsley. Bake uncovered for 10 minutes in the preheated oven. Arrange the cooked mussels, angler fish, scallops and shrimp in a serving dish and sprinkle with the remaining lemon juice and olive oil. Season with salt and pepper, sprinkle with the rest of the parsley and refrigerate until required.

# PEPERONI E MELANZANE RIPIENI
*Stuffed sweet peppers and eggplants*

**1** Cut the eggplants and sweet peppers in half lengthways. Scoop out the eggplant flesh, chop it roughly and sauté in 2 tablespoons of the oil until golden and soft. Remove the seeds and stalks from the sweet peppers.

**3** Lightly oil a large shallow ovenproof dish with a little of the olive oil. Fill the eggplant and sweet pepper shells with the breadcrumb mixture, smoothing the surface of each one. Arrange them in the oiled ovenproof dish.

**2** In a bowl, mix together the chopped tomatoes, anchovies, garlic, basil or marjoram and parsley. Add ½ cup of the grated cheese, the pine nuts and breadcrumbs and the sautéed eggplant mixture. Season to taste with salt and pepper.

PREPARATION: 20 MINUTES
COOKING: 50 MINUTES
SERVES: 4

| |
| --- |
| 2 eggplants |
| 1 large sweet yellow pepper |
| 1 large sweet red pepper |
| 7 tablespoons olive oil |
| 1 pound large tomatoes, skinned and chopped |
| 2 ounces canned anchovy fillets, drained and chopped |
| 2 garlic cloves, minced |
| 2 tablespoons chopped fresh basil or marjoram |
| 2 tablespoons chopped fresh parsley |
| ¾ cup grated Pecorino or Parmesan cheese |
| 2 tablespoons pine nuts |
| 1 cup fresh white breadcrumbs |
| salt and pepper |

**4** Sprinkle with the remaining grated cheese and dribble the rest of the olive oil over the top. Bake in a preheated oven at 400° for 50 minutes or until golden brown. You can serve the sweet peppers and eggplants hot or cold. Either way, they are equally delicious.

# FRITTATA
*Vegetable omelet*

3 tablespoons olive oil

2 onions, very thinly sliced

3 zucchini, thinly sliced

3 tomatoes, skinned and chopped

6 large eggs

salt and freshly ground black pepper

½ cup grated Parmesan cheese

few fresh basil leaves, chopped

1 tablespoon chopped fresh parsley

2 tablespoons butter

**To serve:**

grated Parmesan cheese

**1** Heat the olive oil in a large skillet. Add the sliced onions and sauté very gently for 8-10 minutes until really soft, golden brown and almost caramelized. Add the zucchini and continue cooking until golden on both sides, stirring from time to time. Add the tomatoes and cook over moderate heat until the mixture is thick.

**2** Break the eggs into a large bowl and add the seasoning, grated Parmesan cheese, chopped basil and parsley. Beat well with a wire whisk until they are thoroughly blended.

**3** Drain off and discard any excess oil from the cooked tomato mixture. Add the mixture to the beaten eggs and stir together gently until they are well mixed.

**4** Heat the butter in a large clean skillet until it is hot and sizzling. Pour in the egg mixture and reduce the heat to a bare simmer (as low as it will go). Cook very gently until the omelet is firm and set underneath. Place under a preheated hot broiler for a few seconds to set and brown the top. Slide out on to a plate, and serve at room temperature cut into wedges and sprinkled with grated Parmesan cheese.

PREPARATION: 25 MINUTES
COOKING: 10 MINUTES
SERVES: 4

# ANTIPASTO
*Sweet pepper salad and leeks in vinaigrette*

**1** Place the sweet peppers under a hot broiler and cook them until they are black and blistered. Turn occasionally to cook them evenly on all sides. Place in a polythene bag until cool, and then peel away the skins.

**2** Cut the sweet peppers open and remove the seeds. Cut the flesh into thin strips and arrange in a serving dish. Sprinkle with olive oil and scatter with parsley and garlic. Finally, grind a little sea salt over the top.

**3** Cook the leeks in a large saucepan of lightly salted boiling water for about 10 minutes, or until they are tender but still firm. Drain them thoroughly and then transfer the cooked leeks to a serving dish.

| **For the sweet pepper salad:** |
| --- |
| 4 sweet red, green and yellow peppers |
| 4 tablespoons olive oil |
| 1 tablespoon chopped fresh parsley |
| 2 garlic cloves, minced or chopped |
| freshly ground sea salt |

| **For the leeks in vinaigrette:** |
| --- |
| 1 pound thin leeks, washed and trimmed |
| 6 tablespoons olive oil |
| 1 tablespoon lemon juice |
| 2 tablespoons balsamic or wine vinegar |
| 2 garlic cloves, minced |
| salt and freshly ground black pepper |

**4** Mix together the olive oil, lemon juice, vinegar, garlic and seasoning until well blended. Pour the dressing over the leeks and serve warm or cold with the sweet pepper salad and some fresh ciabatta or crusty bread.

PREPARATION: 30 MINUTES
COOKING: 10 MINUTES
SERVES: 4-6

# COZZE GRATINATE
*Broiled mussels*

4 pounds fresh mussels in their shells

$^3/_4$ cup white wine

$^1/_2$ sweet red pepper, seeded, and chopped

2 garlic cloves, minced

4 tablespoons finely chopped parsley

$1^1/_2$ cups chopped tomatoes, drained

5 tablespoons fresh white breadcrumbs

2 tablespoons olive oil

salt and freshly ground black pepper

1 tablespoon grated Parmesan cheese

1 Put the mussels in a large bowl, cover with cold water and discard any that are open or cracked or rise to the top. Scrub them well under running cold water to clean them thoroughly. Put the cleaned mussels in a large saucepan with the wine and bring to the boil, covered with a closely fitting lid.

3 In a bowl, mix together the chopped sweet pepper, garlic, parsley, chopped tomatoes and 4 tablespoons of the breadcrumbs. Stir in 1 tablespoon of the olive oil and then season to taste with a little salt and some freshly ground black pepper.

4 Add a little of this mixture to each of the mussels in their shells and place them in an ovenproof dish. Sprinkle with grated Parmesan and the remaining breadcrumbs and olive oil and bake in a preheated oven at 450° for 10 minutes. Preheat the broiler and flash the mussels under the hot broiler for a crisp finish.

2 Cook the mussels over medium heat for a few minutes, still covered, and shaking the pan occasionally until the mussels open. Discard any mussels that do not open. Remove the open mussels from the pan and take off and throw away the top half of each shell.

PREPARATION: 30 MINUTES
COOKING: 10 MINUTES
SERVES: 4-6

# FETTUCCINE AL SUGO DI POMODORO

*Fettuccine with tomato sauce*

4 tablespoons olive oil

2 onions, chopped

2 garlic cloves, minced

1 pound plum tomatoes, skinned and chopped

2 tablespoons tomato paste

1 teaspoon sugar

1/3 cup dry white wine

a few ripe olives, pitted and quartered

a handful of torn basil leaves

salt and freshly ground pepper

3/4 pound dried fettuccine

1/2 cup grated Parmesan cheese

**3** Meanwhile, add the fettuccine to a large pan of boiling salted water (to which a little oil has been added to prevent the pasta from sticking). Boil rapidly until the fettuccine is tender but still firm (*al dente,* or "firm to the bite").

**2** Add the tomatoes and tomato paste together with the sugar and wine, stirring well. Cook over gentle heat until the mixture is quite thick and reduced. Stir in the quartered olives and torn basil leaves and season to taste with salt and plenty of freshly ground black pepper.

**1** Heat 3 tablespoons of the olive oil in a large skillet. Add the onions and garlic, and sauté gently over low heat until they are tender and slightly colored. Stir the mixture occasionally.

**4** Drain the fettuccine immediately, mixing in the remaining olive oil and a generous grinding of black pepper. Arrange the pasta on 4 serving plates and top with the tomato sauce, mixing it into the fettuccine. Serve sprinkled with Parmesan cheese.

PREPARATION: 10 MINUTES
COOKING: 20 MINUTES
SERVES: 4

# PASTA ASCIUTTA
*Fresh homemade pasta*

2½ cups strong all-purpose flour, sifted

pinch of salt

3 eggs

1 tablespoon olive oil

flour for dusting

**To serve:**

olive oil

finely minced garlic

salt and freshly ground black pepper

finely chopped fresh parsley

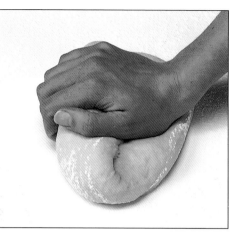

**2** Turn the dough out on to a lightly floured surface and knead well until it is really smooth and silky.

**3** Roll out the dough, giving it an occasional quarter-turn and stretching it out, until it resembles a thin sheet of cloth and is almost transparent. Hang the pasta over the back of a chair or a broom handle and leave for about 10 minutes to dry.

**1** Put the flour and salt on a work surface. Make a well in the center and add the eggs. Using your fingertips, draw the flour in from the sides and mix well. Add the olive oil and continue mixing until you have a soft dough. Alternatively, you can make the dough in a food processor.

**4** Roll the pasta up loosely and then cut through horizontally at regular intervals to make fettuccine (⅛-inch wide) or tagliatelle (¼-inch wide). Unravel them and toss gently in a little flour. Leave them to dry on a cloth for at least 30 minutes before cooking in salted boiling water. Serve with a sauce or simply tossed with olive oil, garlic, salt and pepper and parsley.

PREPARATION: 1 HOUR
COOKING: 2-3 MINUTES
SERVES: 4

**Note:** To make lasagne or ravioli, cut into sheets rather than strips.

# CANNELLONI
*Baked stuffed pasta rolls*

| 8 fresh pasta sheets (about 8 x 5 inches) |
| --- |
| 1 tablespoon vegetable oil |
| 2 tablespoons grated Parmesan cheese |
| 1 tablespoon butter |

**For the filling:**

| 2 tablespoons olive oil |
| --- |
| $^1/_4$ cup chopped onion |
| 1 garlic clove, minced |
| $^1/_2$ pound ground beef |
| 2 tomatoes, skinned, seeded and chopped |
| 1 tablespoon fine breadcrumbs |
| 2 tablespoons grated Parmesan cheese |
| $^1/_4$ teaspoon dried marjoram |
| 1 egg, lightly beaten |
| salt and freshly ground black pepper |

**For the sauce:**

| 3 tablespoons butter |
| --- |
| $^1/_3$ cup flour |
| $1^1/_4$ cups hot milk |
| $^2/_3$ cup hot light cream or half-and-half |
| salt and pepper |
| ground nutmeg |

**1** Make the filling: heat the oil in a saucepan, add the onion and garlic and sauté for 5 minutes until soft. Add the ground beef and cook, stirring, until browned. Add the tomatoes, cover and cook for 10 minutes over low heat. Remove the pan from the heat and stir in the breadcrumbs, cheese, marjoram, egg and seasoning. Set aside to cool.

**2** Make the sauce: melt the butter in a saucepan and stir in the flour. Cook gently over low heat for 1 minute, stirring well. Remove from the heat and whisk in the milk and cream. Return to the heat and bring to the boil, whisking all the time, until thick and smooth. Season with salt, pepper and nutmeg to taste. Cover and keep warm.

**3** Cook the pasta sheets with the oil in a large saucepan of salted boiling water for a few minutes, until tender but *al dente*. Remove the cooked pasta sheets with a slotted spoon and drain well.

**4** Spoon a little of the filling down one long side of each sheet of pasta. Roll each one up into a cylinder. Arrange the cylinders side by side in a well-buttered ovenproof dish. Spoon the sauce over the top to cover the pasta completely. Sprinkle with Parmesan cheese, dot with butter and then bake in a preheated oven at 375° for 20-30 minutes until bubbling and golden.

PREPARATION: 30 MINUTES
COOKING: 20-30 MINUTES
SERVES: 4

# SPAGHETTI ALLA CARBONARA
*Spaghetti with bacon and egg sauce*

**1** Bring a pan of salted water to the boil, adding a little oil if wished to prevent the spaghetti from sticking together. When the water reaches a rolling boil, add the spaghetti to the pan and continue boiling until it is cooked through but still firm to the bite *(al dente)*. Drain well.

**4** Toss the spaghetti mixture lightly with most of the Parmesan cheese and serve immediately while still very hot, sprinkled with the remaining Parmesan cheese and the chopped parsley.

**2** While the spaghetti is cooking, chop the bacon slices into small pieces and sauté in the olive oil in a large saucepan until cooked and golden brown.

| 1 pound spaghetti |
| 8 bacon slices |
| 2 tablespoons olive oil |
| 3 eggs, beaten |
| salt and freshly ground black pepper |
| 3 tablespoons light cream |
| 1/2 cup grated Parmesan cheese |
| 2 tablespoons chopped fresh parsley |

**3** Add the drained cooked spaghetti to the pan and gently stir in the beaten eggs, salt and freshly ground black pepper and cream. Stir very gently over a low heat until the egg starts to set.

PREPARATION: 5 MINUTES
COOKING: 15-20 MINUTES
SERVES: 4

# FETTUCCINE AL PESTO

*Pasta with basil sauce*

**1** Spread the pine nuts out on a baking sheet and place in a preheated oven at 425° for 3-5 minutes, until golden. Keep checking them to make sure that they do not burn.

**3** Tear the basil leaves into shreds and add to the pine nut mixture in the mortar, blender or food processor. Continue pounding or processing until you have a thick green paste. Transfer to a bowl (if using a mortar) and stir in the Parmesan cheese and lemon juice. Add the olive oil, a little at a time, beating well in between each addition.

| | |
|---|---|
| ½ cup pine nuts | |
| 1 garlic clove, minced | |
| 2 ounces fresh basil leaves | |
| ⅔ cup grated Parmesan cheese | |
| juice of ½ lemon | |
| ½ cup olive oil | |
| salt and freshly ground black pepper | |
| 1 pound fettuccine | |
| **To serve:** | |
| ½ cup grated Parmesan cheese | |

**2** Put the pine nuts with the garlic in a mortar and pound the mixture to a thick paste. Alternatively, you can use a blender or food processor for this.

**4** Bring a pan of salted water to the boil and add the fettuccine. Cook until just tender and *al dente* (literally "to the bite") and drain well. Sprinkle with freshly ground black pepper and toss the pasta lightly with the pesto sauce. Serve sprinkled with Parmesan cheese.

PREPARATION: 15-20 MINUTES
COOKING: 5-12 MINUTES
SERVES: 4

# LINGUINE ALLA MARINARA

*Linguine with mussels and tomato sauce*

**3** Add the shelled mussels and mix gently into the tomato sauce. Simmer the mixture over low heat for 2-3 minutes, or until the mussels are heated through.

**1** Prepare the mussels: cover them with cold water and discard any that open or float to the surface. Scrub the remaining mussels to clean them. Place in a large saucepan with ⅓ cup water, cover with a lid and cook over moderate heat until the mussels open, shaking the pan occasionally. Drain the mussels and remove the shells, leaving a few in their shells for decoration.

| 4 pounds fresh mussels in their shells |
| --- |
| 3 tablespoons olive oil |
| 1 onion, chopped |
| 3 garlic cloves, minced |
| 1½ pounds tomatoes, skinned and chopped |
| salt and freshly ground black pepper |
| 1 pound linguine |
| 3 tablespoons chopped parsley |

**2** Heat the olive oil in a skillet and add the onion and garlic. Sauté over medium heat until golden and tender. Add the chopped tomatoes and seasoning, and cook gently over low heat until the mixture is thickened and reduced.

**4** Meanwhile, cook the linguine in salted boiling water until tender (*al dente*). Drain well and gently toss with the tomato and mussel sauce. Transfer to a serving dish or 4 warm plates, sprinkle with chopped parsley and garnish with the reserved mussels.

PREPARATION: 25 MINUTES
COOKING: 20 MINUTES
SERVES: 4

# RAVIOLI DI SPINACI E RICOTTA

*Spinach and ricotta ravioli*

homemade pasta dough
(see page 26)

**For the filling:**

½ pound spinach leaves

½ cup fresh ricotta cheese

¼ cup grated Parmesan cheese

salt and freshly ground black pepper

ground nutmeg

1 egg, beaten

**To serve:**

¼ cup butter, melted

3-4 fresh sage leaves, torn

grated Parmesan cheese

**2** Put the ricotta and Parmesan cheeses in a bowl and mix in the chopped spinach. Add the seasoning, ground nutmeg and beaten egg, mixing well to a paste.

**3** Roll out the pasta as thinly as possible on a lightly floured surface and cut into 2 equal-sized pieces. Put teaspoons of the ricotta and spinach filling over one piece of pasta at intervals, about 2 inches apart.

**4** Cover with the other sheet of pasta and press gently around each little mound with your fingers. Using a pastry cutter wheel, cut the pasta into squares. Cook the ravioli in gently boiling water for 4–5 minutes, until they rise to the surface. Drain and serve with melted butter, sprinkled with sage and Parmesan cheese.

**1** Make the filling: wash the spinach leaves and remove the stalks. Put the spinach in a saucepan without any water, cover with a lid and cook over very low heat for 5 minutes. Drain the spinach and press down firmly with a plate to squeeze out any excess moisture. Roughly chop the drained spinach.

PREPARATION: 25 MINUTES
COOKING: 4-5 MINUTES
SERVES: 4-6

# SPAGHETTI ALLA BOLOGNESE
## *Spaghetti with meat sauce*

1 Make the sauce: heat the oil in a saucepan or deep skillet and sauté the onion, garlic, bacon, carrot and celery until soft and golden. Add the beef and cook, stirring occasionally, until browned.

3 Add the milk and a little ground nutmeg and stir well. Continue cooking until the milk has been absorbed by the meat mixture. Add the tomatoes, sugar and oregano. Reduce the heat to a bare simmer and cook, uncovered, for 2-2$^1$/$_2$ hours until the sauce is reduced and richly colored.

| |
| --- |
| 1 pound spaghetti |
| 1 teaspoon olive oil |
| freshly ground black pepper |
| $^1$/$_2$ cup grated Parmesan cheese |
| **For the bolognese sauce:** |
| 4 tablespoons olive oil |
| 1 onion, finely chopped |
| 1 garlic clove, minced |
| 4 bacon slices, rind removed and chopped |
| 1 carrot, diced |
| 1 celery stick, diced |
| 1 pound ground lean beef |
| $^2$/$_3$ cup red wine |
| salt and freshly ground black pepper |
| $^1$/$_2$ cup milk |
| ground nutmeg |
| 1$^3$/$_4$ cups canned chopped tomatoes |
| 1 tablespoon sugar |
| 1 teaspoon chopped fresh oregano |

2 Add the red wine and bring to the boil. Reduce the heat slightly and cook over medium heat until most of the wine has evaporated. Season with salt and freshly ground black pepper.

PREPARATION: 10 MINUTES
COOKING: 2$^1$/$_2$-3 HOURS
SERVES: 4

4 Bring a large saucepan of salted water to the boil. Add the spaghetti and olive oil and cook until tender but *al dente* (firm to the bite). Drain well and season with freshly ground black pepper. Serve with the bolognese sauce, sprinkled with Parmesan cheese.

# LASAGNE AL FORNO
*Baked layered pasta*

**1** Make the Bolognese meat sauce as per the instructions on page 110. Simmer gently for at least 1 hour until it is time to assemble the lasagne.

**2** Make the white sauce: melt the butter in a saucepan and stir in the flour. Cook over gentle heat, without browning, for 2-3 minutes, and then gradually beat in the milk until you have a thick, smooth, glossy sauce. Season with salt, pepper and nutmeg, and cook gently for 5-10 minutes.

PREPARATION: 1¼ HOURS
COOKING: 30 MINUTES
SERVES: 4

**3** If you are using dried lasagne, drop it into boiling salted water and cook until just tender. Drain and pat dry. Put a little of the meat sauce in a buttered ovenproof dish and cover with a layer of lasagne and then another layer of meat sauce topped with some white sauce. Continue layering up the sauce in this way ending with a layer of lasagne and a topping of white sauce.

| |
|---|
| Bolognese meat sauce (see page 110) |
| ½ pound dried lasagne sheets or freshly made lasagne |
| ⅓ cup grated Parmesan cheese |
| 1 tablespoon butter |
| **For the white sauce:** |
| 3 tablespoons butter |
| 4½ tablespoons flour |
| 2½ cups milk |
| salt and freshly ground black pepper |
| pinch of ground nutmeg |

**4** Sprinkle with grated Parmesan cheese and then dot the top with butter. Bake in a preheated oven at 450° for 30 minutes until the lasagne is golden brown and bubbling. Serve hot with a green salad.

# RISOTTO CON PORCINI

*Mushroom risotto*

1 Heat half of the butter in a large heavy skillet, add the onion and fry gently until it is soft and translucent. Take care that it does not become too colored.

2 Add the sliced mushrooms and cook for 2-3 minutes, stirring occasionally. Add the rice and stir over moderately low heat until all the grains are glistening and beginning to turn translucent around the edges.

3 Stir in a ladleful of boiling stock and simmer very gently until it has been absorbed. Continue adding more stock in this manner until the rice is thoroughly cooked and tender and all the liquid has been absorbed. This will take about 15-20 minutes. Halfway through cooking, stir in the saffron. Stir frequently to prevent the rice sticking to the base of the skillet, and season with salt and pepper.

| |
|---|
| $1/2$ cup butter |
| 1 onion, finely chopped |
| $3/4$ pound mushrooms, thinly sliced |
| $2^1/2$ cups risotto rice, e.g. Arborio |
| 5 cups boiling stock |
| $1/8$ teaspoon powdered saffron or saffron strands |
| salt and freshly ground black pepper |
| $1/3$ cup grated Parmesan cheese |
| **To serve:** |
| 2 tablespoons chopped parsley |
| freshly grated Parmesan cheese |

4 When the rice is ready, gently mix in the remaining butter and the Parmesan cheese. The risotto should not be too dry – in fact, it should be quite moist. Serve the risotto sprinkled with parsley and some more grated Parmesan cheese.

PREPARATION: 5 MINUTES
COOKING: 30 MINUTES
SERVES: 4

# RISOTTO ALLA MARINARA

*Seafood risotto*

**1** Scrub the mussels thoroughly under running cold water and discard any that are cracked. Place in a large saucepan with a little water, and boil, covered, until they open. Shake the pan occasionally. Strain and set aside, retaining the cooking liquid.

**2** Heat the olive oil in a large deep skillet. Add the onion and garlic and fry gently until they are soft and golden, stirring occasionally.

**3** Stir in the rice and cook over low heat for 1-2 minutes, stirring until the grains are glistening with oil and almost translucent. Pour in some of the fish stock and the reserved mussel liquid and wine, and bring to the boil.

| |
|---|
| 1 pound fresh mussels in their shells |
| 4 tablespoons olive oil |
| 1 onion, chopped |
| 2 garlic cloves, minced |
| 2 cups Arborio risotto rice |
| 7 cups fish stock or clam juice |
| ½ cup dry white wine |
| few strands of saffron |
| ¾ pound peeled cooked shrimp |
| ½ pound shucked scallops |
| ½ pound prepared squid |
| salt and freshly ground black pepper |
| 2 tablespoons chopped fresh parsley |
| **To garnish:** |
| sprigs of fresh oregano |

**4** Meanwhile, soak the saffron in a little boiling water and add to the risotto with the prepared shrimp, scallops and squid. Reduce the heat to a simmer and cook gently, adding more fish stock as necessary, until the rice is tender and creamy and all the liquid has been absorbed. Stir in the mussels and season with salt and pepper. Sprinkle with parsley and serve garnished with oregano.

PREPARATION: 25 MINUTES
COOKING: 45 MINUTES
SERVES: 4-6

# SUPPLI ALLA ROMANA

*Stuffed rice croquettes*

**1** Bring 2¹/₂ cups water to the boil in a large pan. Stir in the gravy, tomatoes and butter, and add the rice. Mix well and simmer over low heat for 15 minutes, until the rice is tender. Stir occasionally to prevent it from sticking and add more water if necessary.

**2** Meanwhile, sauté the ham and onion in the butter. Add the veal and cook until lightly browned. Add the tomatoes and simmer until reduced. Add the chicken livers and cook quickly. Season.

**3** Remove the rice mixture from the heat, and stir in the grated cheese and beaten eggs. Season with salt and pepper. Turn the rice mixture out into a bowl and set aside to cool.

| ²/₃ cup left-over meat gravy |
| 3 tomatoes, skinned, seeded and chopped |
| ¹/₄ cup butter |
| 2¹/₂ cups Arborio risotto rice |
| 6 tablespoons grated Parmesan cheese |
| 3 eggs, lightly beaten |
| salt and freshly ground black pepper |
| ¹/₄ pound Mozzarella cheese, diced |
| fine dry breadcrumbs |
| oil for deep-frying |

**For the meat filling:**

| 2 slices Parma ham (prosciutto crudo), shredded |
| 1 small onion, finely chopped |
| ¹/₄ cup butter |
| ¹/₄ pound chopped veal |
| 2 tomatoes, skinned, seeded and chopped |
| ¹/₄ pound chopped chicken livers |
| salt and pepper |

**4** Put a rounded tablespoon of rice in the palm of one hand. Make a depression in the center and fill with some of the meat mixture and 2 cubes of Mozzarella. Cover the filling with the rice and shape into a ball. Repeat with the rest of the mixture and coat the rice balls with breadcrumbs. Deep-fry in hot oil, a few at a time, until golden brown. Drain on paper towels and serve hot.

PREPARATION: 20 MINUTES
COOKING: 45 MINUTES
SERVES: 4-6

# PIZZA NAPOLETANA
*Neapolitan-style pizza*

| |
| --- |
| ½ package active dry yeast |
| 2 tablespoons warm water |
| 2 cups strong all-purpose flour |
| 1 teaspoon salt |
| 2 tablespoons olive oil |
| 3 tablespoons milk |
| **For the topping:** |
| 4 tablespoons olive oil |
| 1½ cups chopped tomatoes |
| salt and freshly ground black pepper |
| 1 tablespoon chopped fresh basil |
| 1 teaspoon dried oregano |
| 6 ounces Mozzarella cheese, sliced |
| 4 tablespoons grated Parmesan cheese |

**1** Blend the yeast with the warm water in a small bowl. Leave in a warm place for 10 minutes until frothy. Sift the flour and salt into a large bowl, make a well in the center and pour in the yeast mixture, oil and milk. Gradually draw the flour into the liquid and mix to form a stiff but pliable dough, adding more milk if necessary.

**3** Roll out the dough to cover two 9-inch or four 6-inch lightly oiled ovenproof plates or pizza pans. Alternatively, place a piece of dough on each plate and press it out, with floured knuckles, to cover the base.

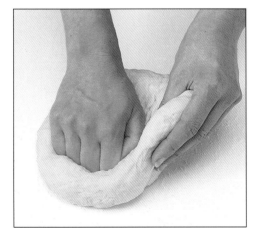

**2** Knead the dough on a lightly floured surface for about 5 minutes until it is light and elastic. Place in an oiled polythene bag and leave in a warm place for 1 hour, or until doubled in size. Turn out onto a floured surface and divide into 2 or 4 pieces. Knead each piece lightly.

**4** Brush with some of the oil, cover with the tomatoes and season with salt and pepper. Sprinkle with basil and oregano and top with Mozzarella. Sprinkle with Parmesan and a little oil. Leave to rise in a warm place for 30 minutes. Bake in a preheated oven at 425° for 15 minutes, then reduce the heat to 350° for 5 minutes. Serve immediately.

PREPARATION: 2 HOURS
COOKING: 20 MINUTES
SERVES: 4

# PESCE SPADA ALLA PALERMITAN

*Swordfish Palermo-style*

4 swordfish steaks, about ½ pound each

salt

flour

2 garlic cloves

½ cup olive oil

4 anchovy fillets, finely chopped

1 onion, finely chopped

4 tomatoes, skinned, seeded and chopped

pinch of dried rosemary, crumbled

12 green olives, pitted and sliced

1 tablespoon capers

freshly ground black pepper

2 tablespoons chopped fresh parsley

**2** Fry the garlic cloves in the olive oil over low heat until golden. Discard the garlic and brown the swordfish steaks in the same oil, turning once. Remove and keep warm.

**3** Add the anchovies and onion to the oil and fry until golden, and the anchovies are reduced to a purée. Add the tomatoes and rosemary and simmer gently for 30 minutes, until reduced and thickened.

**1** Wash the swordfish steaks and pat them dry with paper towels. Sprinkle them with salt and then dust lightly with flour on both sides.

**4** Add the olives and capers and season to taste with salt and pepper. Return the swordfish to the sauce and then heat through very gently. Serve them sprinkled with chopped parsley.

PREPARATION: 15 MINUTES
COOKING: 45 MINUTES
SERVES: 4

# FRITTO MISTO DI MARE
*Fried mixed seafood*

1. Make the batter: sift the flour and salt into a mixing bowl and make a well in the center. Pour in the olive oil and gradually beat in the tepid water to make a smooth, thick batter. Cover the bowl and put in the refrigerator to rest for 2 hours.

2. Immediately before using, whisk the egg white until it forms stiff peaks, and lightly fold the beaten egg white into the batter with a metal spoon. Take care not to beat it into the batter mixture.

PREPARATION: 15 MINUTES
+ 2 HOURS CHILLING TIME
COOKING: 3-6 MINUTES
SERVES: 4

3. Meanwhile, prepare the seafood: wash all the fish and shellfish under running cold water and pat dry. Clean the scallops. Cut the white fish into smallish pieces, and remove any skin and bones. Shell the shrimp, leaving the tails intact and removing the black vein running along the back. Dip them in the prepared batter and shake off any excess batter.

| |
| --- |
| 1 cup all-purpose flour |
| salt |
| 2 tablespoons olive oil |
| ²⁄₃ cup tepid water |
| 1 egg white |
| 2 pounds mixed seafood, e.g. shucked scallops, white fish fillets, jumbo shrimp |
| oil for deep-frying |
| sea salt |
| **For the garnish:** |
| lemon wedges |
| sprigs of parsley |

4. Heat the oil for deep-frying to 375°. Cook the battered fish, scallops and shrimp for 3-6 minutes, depending on size, or until they are crisp and golden. Lift out and drain on crumpled paper towels. Sprinkle with sea salt and pile up on a warm serving dish. Garnish with lemon wedges and parsley and serve immediately.

# SOGLIOLE ALLA PARMIGIANA
*Sole with Parmesan cheese*

**1** Skin the Dover soles. Put some flour in a shallow bowl and season with salt and pepper. Dip the soles into the seasoned flour to dust them lightly on both sides. Shake off any excess flour.

**2** Heat the butter in a large skillet. Add the floured Dover soles and cook over gentle heat until they are golden brown on both sides, turning them once during cooking.

**3** Sprinkle the grated Parmesan cheese over the soles, and then cook very gently for another 2-3 minutes until the cheese melts.

**4** Add the fish stock and the Marsala or white wine. Cover the skillet and cook over very low heat for 4-5 minutes, until the soles are cooked and tender and the sauce reduced. Serve sprinkled with grated Parmesan, garnished with lemon wedges.

PREPARATION: 5 MINUTES
COOKING: 12 MINUTES
SERVES: 4

| |
| --- |
| 4 Dover soles or small flounder |
| flour for dusting |
| salt and freshly ground black pepper |
| 1/3 cup butter |
| 1/4 cup grated Parmesan cheese |
| 1/4 cup fish stock or clam juice |
| 3 tablespoons Marsala or white wine |
| **To serve:** |
| grated Parmesan cheese |
| lemon wedges |

# PESCE ALLA PIZZAIOLA

*Fish with tomato and garlic sauce*

4 x 5-ounce white fish steaks, e.g. striped bass, halibut or angler fish

3 tablespoons olive oil

**For the marinade:**

5 tablespoons olive oil

juice of ½ lemon

1 tablespoon finely chopped fresh parsley

**For the tomato sauce:**

2 tablespoons olive oil

4 garlic cloves, minced

1½ pounds tomatoes, skinned and chopped

4 anchovy fillets, chopped

salt and freshly ground black pepper

1 tablespoon chopped oregano

**1** Wash the fish steaks under running cold water and pat dry with paper towels. Put all the marinade ingredients in a bowl and mix well together.

**2** Add the white fish steaks to the marinade, turning them until they are thoroughly coated and glistening with oil. Cover the bowl and leave in a cool place for at least 1 hour.

**3** Heat the olive oil in a large skillet. Remove the fish steaks from the marinade and fry gently until they are cooked and golden brown on both sides, turning the fish once during cooking. Remove the steaks from the skillet and keep them warm.

**4** While the fish steaks are cooking, make the tomato sauce. Heat the olive oil and sauté the garlic until just golden. Add the tomatoes and chopped anchovies, and cook over medium heat until the tomatoes are reduced to a thick pulpy consistency. Season to taste with salt and pepper. Pour the sauce over the fish and serve sprinkled with oregano.

PREPARATION: 15 MINUTES +
1 HOUR MARINATING
COOKING: 15 MINUTES
SERVES: 4

# TONNO FRESCO ALLA MARINARA

*Fresh tuna with tomatoes*

4 fresh tuna steaks, about 5 ounces each

salt and freshly ground black pepper

flour for dusting

3 tablespoons olive oil

1 onion, chopped

2 garlic cloves, minced

3 cups skinned and chopped tomatoes

2 tablespoons chopped fresh parsley

few basil leaves, chopped

1 bay leaf

4 anchovy fillets, mashed

8 ripe olives

**2** Heat half of the olive oil in a large shallow skillet and sauté the tuna steaks until golden on one side. Flip them over and cook the other side until golden. Carefully remove them from the skillet and then transfer to a dish and keep warm.

**3** Add the remaining oil to the skillet and sauté the onion and garlic for about 5 minutes, until golden and soft. Add the tomatoes, parsley, basil, bay leaf and mashed anchovies and stir well. Bring to the boil and then continue boiling until the mixture reduces and thickens slightly.

**1** Wash the tuna steaks and pat dry with paper towels. Season with salt and plenty of freshly ground black pepper, and then dust the steaks lightly with flour.

**4** Return the tuna to the skillet, season to taste and simmer gently for 15 minutes, turning once. Turn off the heat, add the olives and leave to stand for 5 minutes. Discard the bay leaf and transfer the tuna steaks in their sauce to a warm serving dish.

PREPARATION: 15 MINUTES
COOKING: 30 MINUTES
SERVES: 4

# PESCE ALLA SICILIANA

*Sicilian fish stew*

**1** Prepare the mussels: cover with cold water and discard any which are cracked or open or float to the top. Scrub well to clean them thoroughly and soak in fresh cold water until ready to cook.

**2** Heat 2 tablespoons of the olive oil in a heavy-based skillet, and sauté the onion, garlic and carrots for about 5 minutes, or until soft. Add the tomatoes with their juice, the ripe olives and bay leaf, and season with salt and freshly ground black pepper. Simmer gently for 15 minutes.

**3** Cut 4 large circles from the slices of bread. Heat the remaining oil in a small skillet and then sauté the bread until crisp and golden on both sides. Remove, drain on paper towels and keep warm.

**4** Add the prepared fish to the stew and cook for 5 minutes. Add the mussels and simmer for 10 minutes, or until the shells open. Discard any that do not open. Remove the bay leaf. Put a fried bread croûte in the bottom of each of 4 warm deep plates or large shallow soup bowls. Ladle the fish stew over the top. Sprinkle with chopped parsley and serve immediately with plenty of crusty bread.

| |
|---|
| ½ pound fresh mussels in their shells |
| ⅓ cup olive oil |
| 1 onion, thinly sliced |
| 2 garlic cloves, minced |
| 2 carrots, cut into strips |
| 1¾ cups canned chopped tomatoes |
| ¼ pound ripe olives |
| 1 bay leaf |
| salt and freshly ground black pepper |
| 4 slices white bread |
| 2 pounds mixed fish, e.g. white fish, goat fish, scallops, shrimp, prepared or cut into chunks |
| 2 tablespoons finely chopped fresh parsley |

PREPARATION: 30 MINUTES
COOKING: 35 MINUTES
SERVES: 4

# TROTA IN CARTOCCIO

*Baked trout parcels*

| |
|---|
| 2 tablespoons olive oil |
| 2 garlic cloves, minced |
| 1 medium onion, chopped |
| 1 celery stick, chopped |
| salt and freshly ground black pepper |
| 4 sprigs of rosemary |
| 2 tablespoons dry white wine |
| 2 x 12-ounce trout, cleaned |

**To garnish:**

| |
|---|
| sprigs of rosemary |

**1** Heat the olive oil in a skillet and add the garlic, onion and celery. Fry gently for about 5 minutes until soft and golden. Add some salt and ground black pepper, 2 rosemary sprigs and the white wine. Cook gently for 5 minutes.

**2** Cut out 2 double sheets of waxed paper large enough to enclose the trout. Brush the paper lightly with a little oil. Divide the sautéed onion mixture equally between the 2 pieces of paper.

**4** Fold the paper over the fish and wrap loosely, securing the sides with a double fold and double folding the ends. Place on a baking sheet and cook in a preheated oven at 350° for 20 minutes until the fish is cooked and tender. Remove the fish from the paper and serve garnished with sprigs of rosemary.

**3** Wash the trout and dry well with paper towels. Sprinkle inside and out with salt and freshly ground black pepper. Place one trout on top of the onion mixture on each piece of paper and top with a sprig of rosemary.

PREPARATION: 10-15 MINUTES
COOKING: 20 MINUTES
SERVES: 2

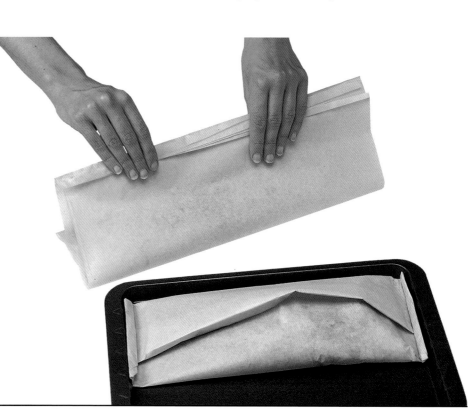

# COZZE ITALIANO

*Mussels Italian-style*

**1** Prepare the mussels: place in a bowl and cover them with cold water. Discard any that are open or rise to the surface. Scrub the mussels to clean them thoroughly. Soak in fresh cold water until ready to cook. Drain well.

**3** Remove the empty half of each mussel shell, and arrange the remaining shells, mussel-side up, close together in a shallow ovenproof baking dish. Sprinkle with the chopped onion, garlic, parsley, breadcrumbs and Parmesan cheese.

**2** Put the mussels in a deep saucepan with the bouquet garni, salt and pepper. Add the water and wine, cover the pan and cook over moderate heat until the mussels open, shaking the pan occasionally. Discard any mussels that do not open, then strain them and reserve the liquid.

| |
|---|
| 4 pounds fresh mussels in their shells |
| bouquet garni |
| salt and freshly ground black pepper |
| 1/2 cup water |
| 1/2 cup dry white wine |
| 2 tablespoons finely chopped onion |
| 1 garlic clove, minced |
| 2 tablespoons chopped fresh parsley |
| 1 1/2 cups fresh breadcrumbs |
| 3 tablespoons grated Parmesan cheese |
| 2 tablespoons butter |

**4** Reduce the mussel liquid to half its original volume by boiling rapidly. Pour the reduced liquid around the mussels and dot with butter. Bake in a preheated oven at 350° for 15 minutes. Serve immediately.

PREPARATION: 30 MINUTES
COOKING: 15 MINUTES
SERVES: 4

# SCALOPPINE ALLA BOLOGNESE

*Veal escalopes Bologna-style*

**1** Beat the escalopes lightly with a rolling pin to thin them out. Sprinkle each one with a little salt and coat them with flour. Preheat the oven to 450°, or the broiler to high.

**3** Cover each escalope with a slice of ham and then top with a slice of cheese. Leave them in a warm place while you deglaze the skillet.

**2** In a large skillet, melt the butter and, when foaming, sauté the escalopes on both sides until they are lightly browned and cooked. Arrange them side by side in a buttered ovenproof dish.

**4** Add the stock and Marsala to the butter in the skillet. Bring to the boil, scraping the residues away from the bottom of the skillet with a wooden spoon. Pour the sauce over the escalopes, sprinkle with black pepper and place the baking dish in the hot oven or under the broiler until the cheese has melted. Serve sprinkled with parsley.

PREPARATION: 10 MINUTES
COOKING: 15–20 MINUTES
SERVES: 4

| |
|---|
| 8 small veal escalopes, about 3 ounces each |
| salt |
| flour for coating |
| $1/3$ cup butter |
| 8 thin slices Parma ham (prosciutto crudo) |
| 8 thin slices Swiss cheese |
| 3 tablespoons chicken stock |
| 3 tablespoons Marsala |
| freshly ground black pepper |
| 2 tablespoons chopped fresh parsley |

# SALTIMBOCCA ALLA ROMANA

*Veal escalopes with Parma ham and sage*

|  |
| --- |
| 8 small veal escalopes, about 2 ounces each |
| 8 paper-thin slices of Parma ham (prosciutto crudo) |
| salt |
| 8 fresh sage leaves |
| 1/3 cup butter |
| 1/3 cup Marsala or dry white wine |
| fresh sage leaves to garnish |

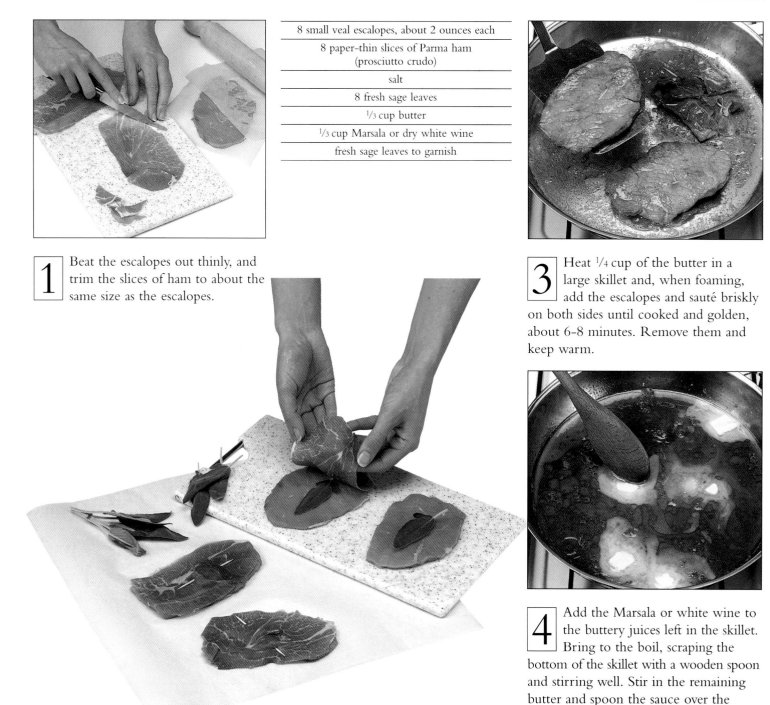

**1** Beat the escalopes out thinly, and trim the slices of ham to about the same size as the escalopes.

**2** Sprinkle each escalope with a pinch of salt and place a sage leaf on top. Cover each escalope with a slice of ham, and secure with a wooden toothpick. Do not roll up.

**3** Heat 1/4 cup of the butter in a large skillet and, when foaming, add the escalopes and sauté briskly on both sides until cooked and golden, about 6-8 minutes. Remove them and keep warm.

**4** Add the Marsala or white wine to the buttery juices left in the skillet. Bring to the boil, scraping the bottom of the skillet with a wooden spoon and stirring well. Stir in the remaining butter and spoon the sauce over the escalopes. Garnish with fresh sage leaves.

PREPARATION: 10 MINUTES
COOKING: 12-15 MINUTES
SERVES: 4

69

# OSSO BUCO ALLA MILANESE

*Braised shin of veal*

| 1 onion, finely chopped |
| 1/2 cup butter |
| 1 meaty shin of veal, sawed into 4 slices, about 2 1/2 inches thick |
| flour for dusting |
| 1 carrot, thinly sliced |
| 1 celery stick, thinly sliced |
| 3 tomatoes, skinned and chopped |
| salt and freshly ground black pepper |
| 2-3 sage leaves |
| 2/3 cup dry white wine |

**For the gremolata:**

| 4 tablespoons finely chopped parsley |
| 1 garlic clove, minced |
| 1 anchovy fillet, finely chopped |
| finely grated peel of 1/2 lemon |

**2** Add the carrot, celery and tomatoes. Season with salt and pepper and add the sage leaves. Stir in the wine, then cover the skillet and simmer gently for about 1 hour, or until the veal is cooked and tender. Add a few tablespoons of water or a little more wine if the sauce evaporates too quickly.

**1** Fry the onion in half of the butter in a wide shallow skillet until it is soft and golden. Dust the slices of veal with flour and then fry them in the same skillet, turning several times, until they are golden brown on all sides. Stand them on their sides to prevent the marrow in the bones from slipping out during cooking.

PREPARATION: 15 MINUTES
COOKING: 2 HOURS
SERVES: 4

**3** While the veal is cooking, prepare the gremolata. Mix together thoroughly the parsley, garlic, anchovy and finely grated lemon peel in a small bowl until well combined.

**4** Spread each piece of veal with a little of the gremolata and cook for a few minutes. Transfer the veal to a heated serving dish and keep warm. Add a few tablespoons of water to the skillet juices and bring to the boil, scraping the bottom of the skillet clean. Simmer until slightly reduced and thickened. Stir in the remaining butter and, when it has melted, pour over the veal. Serve with risotto.

71

# MESSICANI ALLA MILANESE
*Milanese stuffed veal rolls*

12 small thin slices of veal

6 fresh sage leaves

2 bacon slices

1/4 cup butter

4 tablespoons Marsala

4 tablespoons dry white wine

3 fresh sage leaves, roughly chopped

**For the filling:**

2 ounces raw smoked ham
(prosciutto crudo), chopped

1 chicken liver, finely chopped

1/2 cup fresh white breadcrumbs

2 tablespoons freshly grated Parmesan cheese

1 teaspoon finely chopped parsley

1 egg, beaten

salt and freshly ground black pepper

1/4 teaspoon ground nutmeg

**2** Beat the slices of veal flat with a rolling pin. Put some meat mixture on each slice of veal and roll it up. Thread 2 veal rolls on to each of 6 short wooden skewers, together with a sage leaf. Cut each bacon slice into 3 pieces and then thread one on to each skewer.

**1** Make the filling: put the chopped ham, chicken liver, breadcrumbs, Parmesan and parsley in a bowl. Bind together with the beaten egg, and season to taste with salt, pepper and ground nutmeg.

PREPARATION: 15 MINUTES
COOKING: 15 MINUTES
SERVES: 4-6

**3** Heat the butter in a skillet and then sauté the veal rolls until they are evenly cooked and golden brown, turning occasionally. Remove the veal rolls from the skillet and keep warm while you make the sauce.

**4** Add the Marsala and wine to the buttery juices and bring to the boil, scraping the bottom of the skillet clean with a wooden spoon. Add the chopped sage and simmer for 3-5 minutes until reduced slightly. Pour the sauce over the veal rolls and serve immediately.

# BRASATO AL BAROLO

*Beef braised in red wine*

3 pounds eye round roast

1 onion, sliced

1 carrot, sliced

1 celery stick, sliced

2 garlic cloves, minced

2 bay leaves

6 peppercorns

2½ cups Barolo or other red wine

2 tablespoons bacon fat

1 onion, finely chopped

sprig of rosemary

salt and freshly ground black pepper

**1** Put the beef in a deep bowl. Add the sliced onion, carrot, celery, garlic, bay leaves, peppercorns and the red wine. Cover the bowl and place in the refrigerator to marinate for 24 hours, turning the beef several times. Lift the meat out of the marinade and dry it carefully. Reserve the marinade.

**2** Heat the bacon fat in a large flameproof casserole and sauté the chopped onion over low heat for about 5 minutes, or until it is soft and golden. Put in the beef, increase the heat and brown quickly on all sides.

**3** Strain the reserved marinade into the casserole and bring to the boil. Add the rosemary sprig and season with salt and freshly ground black pepper. Lower the heat, cover tightly and simmer very gently for at least 3 hours, or until the meat is tender. Turn the meat once halfway through cooking.

**4** Transfer the meat to a carving dish or board and slice fairly thickly. Arrange the slices on a warm serving dish. If the sauce is too thin, reduce a little by rapid boiling. Remove the rosemary and pour the sauce over the meat. Serve immediately with puréed potatoes and carrots.

PREPARATION: 5 MINUTES + 24 HOURS MARINATING
COOKING: 3¼ HOURS
SERVES: 6

# INVOLTINI AL SUGO

*Stuffed beef olives*

| |
|---|
| 2 pounds eye round roast |
| salt and freshly ground black pepper |
| 1 cup grated Pecorino cheese |
| 2 slices raw ham (prosciutto crudo), chopped |
| 3 garlic cloves, minced |
| 3 tablespoons chopped fresh parsley |
| 1 tablespoon chopped fresh basil |
| 3 tablespoons olive oil |
| few basil leaves, torn |
| **For the tomato sauce:** |
| 1 onion, chopped |
| 2 garlic cloves, minced |
| 2 pounds tomatoes, skinned and chopped |
| 1 tablespoon tomato paste |
| 1/2 cup red wine |
| salt and freshly ground black pepper |

**2** Make the filling: put the grated Pecorino cheese in a bowl with the chopped ham, garlic, parsley and basil. Mix well together and spread a little of this mixture on to each slice of beef. Roll up, folding in the sides, and secure with kitchen string.

**1** Cut the beef into thin slices and place between 2 sheets of waxed paper. Flatten them with a rolling pin and then season with salt and ground black pepper.

PREPARATION: 20 MINUTES
COOKING: 1 1/2 -2 HOURS
SERVES: 6

**3** Heat the olive oil in a large saucepan and gently fry the beef rolls until they are slightly brown all over, turning as necessary. Remove from the pan and keep warm.

**4** Make the sauce: add the onion and garlic to the oil in the pan and sauté until soft. Add the tomatoes, tomato paste, wine and seasoning. Bring to the boil, and then add the beef rolls. Cover and simmer gently for 1 1/2-2 hours, or until tender. Remove the string from the beef rolls and serve with the sauce, sprinkled with basil.

# FEGATO ALLA VENEZIANA

*Calf's liver Venetian-style*

**1** Heat the olive oil and butter together in a large heavy-based skillet. Add the onions and simmer gently over very low heat, stirring occasionally, for about 40 minutes, or until the onions are soft, golden and translucent but not browned. Remove the onions with a slotted spoon and keep warm.

**2** Add the thinly sliced calf's liver to the skillet and fry very quickly until brown on one side. Turn over and quickly cook the other side. The liver should be lightly browned on the outside and still pink in the middle. Remove and keep warm.

**3** Add the veal or chicken stock and vinegar to the skillet and bring to the boil, scraping the bottom of the skillet with a wooden spoon and stirring until the sauce reduces. Season to taste with salt and ground black pepper, and stir in the chopped parsley.

| 6 tablespoons olive oil |
| --- |
| 1 tablespoon butter |
| 4 medium-sized onions, thinly sliced |
| 1¼ pounds calf's liver, thinly sliced |
| 4 tablespoons veal or chicken stock |
| 1 tablespoon wine vinegar |
| salt |
| freshly ground black pepper |
| 2 tablespoons finely chopped parsley |

**4** Arrange the liver and onions on a heated serving dish or 4 serving plates, and pour the sauce over the top. Serve with a bowl of fresh pasta and a crisp green salad.

PREPARATION: 10 MINUTES
COOKING: 50 MINUTES
SERVES: 4

# POLLO ALLA CACCIATORA
*Hunter's chicken*

| |
|---|
| 4 tablespoons olive oil |
| 4 slices pancetta or bacon, chopped |
| 1 large chicken, about 3 pounds, cut into 4 pieces |
| 2 garlic cloves, minced |
| 2 red-skinned onions, roughly chopped |
| 1 pound tomatoes, skinned and chopped |
| ½ pound mushrooms, sliced |
| sprig of rosemary |
| 1 bay leaf |
| ⅔ cup dry white wine |
| 1¼ cups chicken stock |
| salt and pepper |

**2** Put the chicken pieces in the skillet and sauté in the oil, turning occasionally, until they are golden brown all over.

**1** Heat the oil in a large skillet and fry the pancetta or bacon for 2-3 minutes, until lightly browned. Stir occasionally to prevent the pancetta from sticking. Remove and keep warm.

**3** Remove the chicken from the skillet and keep warm. Add the garlic, onions, tomatoes and mushrooms, and cook gently over low heat for 5 minutes, stirring occasionally. Return the chicken to the skillet.

**4** Add the herbs, then pour in the wine and chicken stock. Simmer gently for about 1 hour, until the chicken is tender and the sauce reduced. Season to taste with salt and pepper.

PREPARATION: 15 MINUTES
COOKING: 1¼ HOURS
SERVES: 4

# PETTI DI POLLO RIPIENI

*Stuffed chicken breasts*

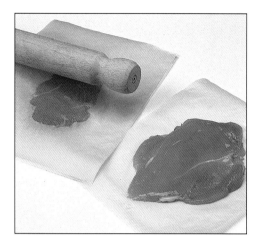

| |
|---|
| 4 chicken breasts, skinned and boned |
| salt and freshly ground black pepper |
| 4 thin small slices Parma ham (prosciutto crudo) |
| 4 thin slices Bel Paese cheese |
| 4 cooked or canned asparagus stalks |
| flour for dusting |
| 1/4 cup butter |
| 1 tablespoon olive oil |
| 6 tablespoons Marsala or dry white wine |
| 2 tablespoons chicken stock |
| **To garnish:** |
| cooked or canned asparagus stalks |

**1** Place each chicken breast between 2 sheets of damp waxed paper and then beat with a rolling pin until thin. Season lightly with salt and freshly ground black pepper.

**2** Place a slice of ham on top of each beaten chicken breast, then a slice of cheese and, finally, an asparagus stalk. Roll each breast up and wind a piece of kitchen string around to hold it. Tie securely and dust with flour.

**3** Heat 2 tablespoons of the butter with the oil in a skillet. Sauté the chicken rolls over very low heat, turning them frequently, for about 15 minutes, or until tender, cooked and golden. Remove the string, and transfer the rolls to a serving dish and keep warm.

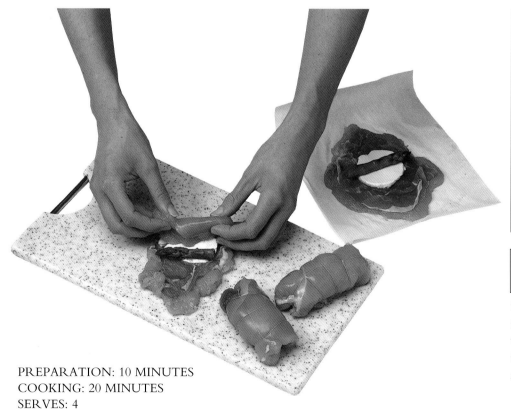

**4** Add the Marsala or wine, chicken stock and the remaining butter to the juices in the skillet. Bring to the boil and simmer for 3-4 minutes, scraping the base of the skillet with a wooden spoon. Spoon the sauce over the chicken and serve garnished with asparagus stalks.

PREPARATION: 10 MINUTES
COOKING: 20 MINUTES
SERVES: 4

# POLLO CON POLENTA

*Tuscan chicken with polenta*

4 tablespoons olive oil

1 chicken, cut up

1 onion, chopped

5 plum tomatoes, skinned and chopped

1¼ cups dry white wine

sprig of rosemary

1 tablespoon chopped fresh thyme

salt and freshly ground black pepper

2 tablespoons flour blended with
1 tablespoon butter

2 tablespoons chopped fresh parsley

**For the polenta:**

7½ cups water

salt

2 cups yellow cornmeal

1 tablespoon butter

freshly ground black pepper

**2** Add the onion to the skillet and cook gently until soft and golden. Add the chopped tomatoes, white wine, rosemary, thyme and salt and pepper. Bring to the boil, stirring, and then reduce the heat to a simmer. Return the chicken to the skillet and then simmer, covered, for 20–30 minutes until the chicken is cooked.

**3** Meanwhile, make the polenta: put the cold water, salt and cornmeal in a large saucepan and stir thoroughly with a wooden spoon. Bring slowly to the boil, stirring continuously, and then reduce the heat to a simmer. Continue stirring over low heat for 15–20 minutes until the polenta is thick and smooth and has absorbed all the liquid. Stir in the butter and season with black pepper.

**1** Heat the olive oil in a large heavy-based skillet and sauté the chicken pieces until golden brown all over, turning occasionally. Remove and keep warm.

**4** Remove the chicken and arrange on a heated serving dish. Add the blended flour and butter (*beurre manié*) to the sauce and bring to the boil, stirring constantly, until the sauce thickens slightly. Pour over the chicken, sprinkle with parsley and serve with the polenta.

PREPARATION: 15 MINUTES
COOKING: 45 MINUTES
SERVES: 4

# PARMIGIANA DI MELANZANE

*Baked eggplants with cheese*

**1** Trim the stems from the eggplants and slice them into rounds – not lengthways. Sprinkle each slice with a little salt and place the salted slices in a colander. Cover with a plate and weight it down. Leave the eggplants to drain for about 30 minutes.

| |
|---|
| 3 pounds eggplants |
| salt |
| 1/2 cup olive oil |
| 1 onion, finely chopped |
| 4 pounds tomatoes, skinned and chopped |
| 3 fresh basil leaves, torn, or 2 teaspoons dried basil |
| freshly ground black pepper |
| flour for dusting |
| 1 cup grated Parmesan cheese |
| 1/2 pound Mozzarella cheese, thinly sliced |

**3** Rinse the eggplant slices thoroughly in cold water to remove the saltiness. Pat dry with paper towels and dust them with flour. Heat a little of the remaining olive oil in a large skillet and fry the eggplant in batches, adding more oil as needed, until they are cooked and golden brown on both sides. Drain on paper towels.

**4** Oil an ovenproof dish and arrange a layer of eggplant slices in the bottom of the dish. Sprinkle with Parmesan cheese and cover with Mozzarella cheese slices. Spoon some of the tomato sauce over the top and continue layering up in this way until all the ingredients are used up, ending with a layer of tomato sauce and Parmesan cheese. Bake in a preheated oven at 400° for 30 minutes. Serve hot, warm or cold.

**2** Meanwhile, make the tomato sauce: heat 4 tablespoons of the olive oil in a heavy pan, and fry the onion until soft and golden. Add the chopped tomatoes and basil, mix well and simmer gently, uncovered, until the mixture reduces to a thick sauce. Season to taste with salt and pepper.

PREPARATION: 40 MINUTES
COOKING: 1 HOUR
SERVES: 4

# ZUCCHINI RIPIENI
*Stuffed zucchini*

**1** Trim the ends from the zucchini and cook in a large saucepan of boiling salted water for 5 minutes. Drain well. Soak the bread in a little milk until soft and then squeeze dry.

| |
| --- |
| 6 medium zucchini |
| salt |
| 1 ounce crustless white bread |
| milk for soaking |
| 1/2 cup ricotta or soft curd cheese |
| 1/4 teaspoon dried oregano |
| 1 garlic clove, minced |
| 1/3 cup grated Parmesan cheese |
| 1 egg yolk |
| freshly ground black pepper |

**4** Arrange the zucchini cases close together in a single layer in a well-oiled shallow baking tray or ovenproof dish. Fill the cases with the ricotta mixture, and bake in a preheated oven at 375° for 35-40 minutes until the zucchini are tender and the filling is golden brown. Serve immediately.

**3** Chop the zucchini centers finely and put into a bowl. Add the bread, ricotta, oregano, garlic, Parmesan, egg yolk, salt and freshly ground black pepper. Mix thoroughly. The consistency should be fairly soft. If it is too stiff, add a little milk.

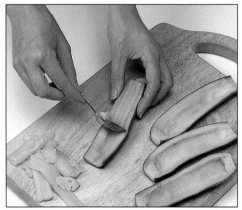

**2** Cut the zucchini in half lengthways and carefully scoop out the centers, using a teaspoon. You should be left with long boat-shaped cases which are ready for filling.

PREPARATION: 20 MINUTES
COOKING: 35-40 MINUTES
SERVES: 4

# CAPONATA

*Sicilian-style eggplants*

1 Put the diced eggplant in a colander, sprinkle with salt and leave to drain for 15-20 minutes to exude their bitter juices. Rinse under running cold water to remove any salt and pat dry with paper towels.

2 Soak the anchovies in a little warm water in a bowl to remove some of their saltiness. Remove, pat dry and cut the anchovies into thin strips. Set aside.

PREPARATION: 40 MINUTES
COOKING: 1 HOUR
SERVES: 4

3 Sauté the onion in the olive oil until soft and golden. Add the celery and cook for a further 2-3 minutes. Add the eggplant and cook gently for 3 minutes, stirring occasionally, until golden. Add the passata and cook gently until it has been absorbed by the eggplant. Add the wine vinegar and cook for 1 minute.

| |
| --- |
| 3 eggplants cut into $\frac{1}{2}$-inch dice |
| salt |
| 2 ounces anchovy fillets |
| 1 onion, thinly sliced |
| 4 tablespoons olive oil |
| 2 sticks celery, diced |
| $\frac{2}{3}$ cup passata (sieved tomatoes) |
| 3 tablespoons wine vinegar |
| 1 sweet yellow pepper, seeded and thinly sliced |
| 1 sweet red pepper, seeded and thinly sliced |
| 2 ounces capers, roughly chopped |
| 2 ounces ripe olives, pitted and sliced |
| 2 ounces green olives, pitted and sliced |
| 2 tablespoons pine nuts |
| 2 tablespoons chopped parsley |

Add the sweet peppers, anchovies, capers and olives and cook for 3 minutes.

4 Transfer the mixture to an ovenproof dish and bake, covered, in a preheated oven at 350° for about 1 hour. After 40 minutes, stir in the pine nuts and return to the oven for the remaining 20 minutes. Serve lukewarm or cold sprinkled with chopped parsley. The flavors improve if made a day in advance.

# CROSTATA DI SPINACI

*Savory spinach tart*

**1** Sift the flour and salt into a mixing bowl and rub in the butter. Mix in the egg yolk and sufficient iced water to make a soft dough. Knead lightly until smooth. Leave in the refrigerator for at least 30 minutes to rest. Roll out the pastry to line a 10-inch quiche pan.

**2** Prick the base of the pastry shell with a fork. Fill with waxed paper or foil and baking beans, and bake "blind" in a preheated oven at 400° for 15 minutes. Remove the baking beans and paper and return to the oven for a further 5 minutes to cook the base.

**3** Make the filling: cook the spinach in a little salted water for 3 minutes until softened but still a fresh bright green color. Drain in a colander and squeeze out any excess water by pressing down hard with a plate. Chop the drained spinach.

| 2 cups all-purpose flour |
| pinch of salt |
| ½ cup butter |
| 1 egg yolk |
| 2-3 tablespoons iced water |
| **For the filling:** |
| ½ pound small, tender spinach leaves |
| 1½ cups ricotta cheese |
| 4 eggs, beaten |
| salt and freshly ground black pepper |
| ground nutmeg |
| ⅓ cup light cream |
| ¼ cup grated Parmesan cheese |

**4** Put the ricotta in a bowl and beat in the eggs, salt and pepper and nutmeg. Beat in the cream and continue beating until smooth. Spoon the filling into the pastry shell and smooth the top. Sprinkle with Parmesan cheese and bake at 350° for 30 minutes until risen, set and golden brown.

PREPARATION: 30 MINUTES +
30 MINUTES CHILLING
COOKING: 30 MINUTES
SERVES: 8

# GNOCCHI AL PESTO

*Gnocchi with basil sauce*

**1** Make the pesto: chop the basil and pine nuts roughly and put into a mortar with the garlic, salt and pepper. Pound together until reduced to a thick paste. Transfer to a bowl, add the oil, a little at a time, stirring constantly until thick. Stir in the lemon juice and Parmesan cheese, cover and set aside.

**3** With floured hands, roll small pieces of the dough into small croquettes, about the thickness of your thumb. Press them lightly with the prongs of a fork – this will help them to hold the pesto sauce.

**2** Make the gnocchi: drain the potatoes well and shake over the heat to dry them thoroughly. Mash them very finely so that there are no lumps. Beat in the flour, egg, salt, pepper and nutmeg. Mix to a dough and turn out on to a floured board.

PREPARATION: 25 MINUTES
COOKING: 15 MINUTES
SERVES: 4

| 1 pound potatoes, freshly boiled |
| --- |
| 1½ cups all-purpose flour |
| 1 egg, beaten |
| salt and freshly ground black pepper |
| ground nutmeg |
| **For the pesto sauce:** |
| 2 ounces fresh basil leaves |
| ¼ cup pine nuts |
| 2 garlic cloves |
| salt and freshly ground black pepper |
| 4 tablespoons olive oil |
| juice of ½ lemon |
| ⅓ cup grated Parmesan cheese |
| **To serve:** |
| 2 tablespoons butter |
| grated Parmesan cheese |

**4** Bring some salted water to the boil in a large pan. Drop the gnocchi, a few at a time, into the boiling water and cook for 3-5 minutes. They will rise to the surface and float when they are cooked. Remove and drain. Arrange the gnocchi in a buttered serving dish and dot with butter and sprinkle with Parmesan cheese. Pour the pesto sauce over the top.

# CASSATA ALLA SICILIANA

*Sicilian cheesecake*

| 3 eggs, separated |
| --- |
| ½ cup granulated sugar |
| finely grated peel of ½ lemon |
| 1 cup all-purpose flour |
| 1 teaspoon baking soda |
| **For the filling:** |
| ¾ cup granulated sugar |
| 3 cups ricotta cheese |
| 1 pound mixed candied fruit |
| ⅛ teaspoon ground cinnamon |
| 3 squares semisweet dark chocolate, chopped in small pieces |
| 8 tablespoons Maraschino liqueur |

**1** Make the sponge: whisk the egg yolks with the sugar, lemon peel and 3 tablespoons of hot water until light and foamy. Sift the flour and baking soda together and fold it gently into the egg yolk mixture.

**3** Make the filling: dissolve the sugar in 3 tablespoons of water over low heat. Beat the syrup with the ricotta cheese until well blended. Chop half of the fruit coarsely. Beat the cinnamon into the ricotta mixture, and put aside a few tablespoons for decoration. Stir the chopped fruit and chocolate into the rest of the mixture.

**4** Line the base of the cake pan with waxed paper. Cut the sponge in half horizontally and put one layer on the base, cut-side up. Sprinkle with half of the Maraschino, and spread with the ricotta mixture. Place the other sponge layer on top and sprinkle with the remaining Maraschino. Fit the ring of the pan in position and chill for several hours. To serve, remove from the pan, coat the top and sides with the reserved ricotta mixture and decorate with the reserved whole fruit.

**2** Whisk the egg whites until they are stiff, but not dry. Fold them into the sponge mixture. Pour the mixture into a buttered 10-inch springform cake pan and bake in a preheated oven at 375° for 15-20 minutes, or until the cake is golden and springs back when pressed. Turn out and cool.

PREPARATION: 40 MINUTES
COOKING: 15-20 MINUTES
CHILLING: 2-3 HOURS
SERVES: 6-8

# ZABAGLIONE
### *Whipped wine custard*

1 Separate the eggs and put the egg yolks in the top of a double-boiler, or in a bowl sitting over a small saucepan of gently simmering water. Make sure that the bowl is not in contact with the water below.

2 Add the sugar and Marsala or sweet white wine, if using, to the egg yolks and stir well.

| 4 egg yolks |
| --- |
| 5 tablespoons sugar |
| 8 tablespoons Marsala or sweet white wine |

3 Beat the mixture with either a wire whisk or a hand-held electric whisk until the zabaglione is thick, light and hot. Even with an electric whisk, this will take 10-15 minutes so be patient. Check that the water simmers gently underneath and does not boil dry.

4 When the zabaglione is cooked, pour it carefully into 4 tall glasses and serve immediately. To serve it cold, continue beating the mixture, off the heat, until it has cooled down completely. Mix the cold zabaglione with raspberries or sliced strawberries or peaches if wished.

PREPARATION: 2-3 MINUTES
COOKING: 10-15 MINUTES
SERVES: 4

# PANETTONE
*Italian fruit cake*

**1** Stir 1 teaspoon of the sugar and all of the yeast into the lukewarm water. Leave to stand for about 10 minutes until frothy. Beat the egg yolks in a large bowl and stir in the yeast mixture, salt and remaining sugar. Beat in 2 cups of the flour and then gradually beat in the softened butter, a little at a time. Knead in the remaining flour to make a dough.

**2** Turn the dough out on to a lightly floured surface and knead well until the dough is firm and elastic. Place in a lightly oiled polythene bag and leave in a warm place until well risen and doubled in size.

PREPARATION: 1½ HOURS
COOKING: 40 – 50 MINUTES
SERVES: 10

| |
| --- |
| ¼ cup granulated sugar |
| 1 package active dry yeast |
| ⅔ cup lukewarm water |
| 3 egg yolks |
| salt |
| 3½ cups strong all-purpose flour |
| ½ cup butter, softened |
| ½ cup seedless white raisins |
| ½ cup raisins |
| ⅓ cup chopped mixed candied peel |
| 2 tablespoons melted butter |

**3** Turn the dough out on to a floured surface and knead in the seedless white raisins, raisins and candied peel. Knead until the fruit is evenly distributed. Place the dough in a greased 7-inch round cake pan, and cover with oiled plastic wrap. Leave in a warm place until the dough rises to the top of the pan.

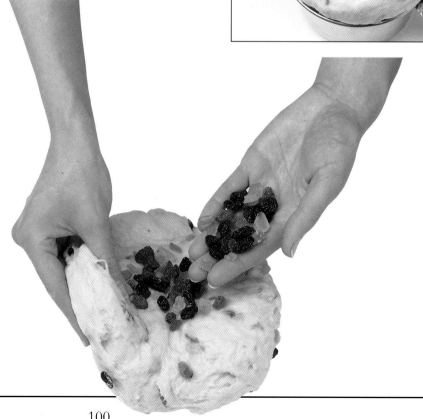

**4** Remove the plastic wrap, and brush the top of the dough with some of the melted butter. Bake in a preheated oven at 400° for 20 minutes. Reduce the oven temperature to 350° and cook for a further 20-30 minutes. Remove from the pan and brush the top and sides of the panettone with the remaining melted butter. Serve warm or cold cut into thin slices.

# CROSTATA DI RICOTTA

*Neapolitan ricotta tart*

| 2 cups all-purpose flour |
| pinch of salt |
| 1/2 cup butter |
| 1 egg yolk |
| 2-3 tablespoons iced water |
| confectioners' sugar for dusting |
| **For the filling:** |
| 1 1/2 cups ricotta cheese |
| 1/3 cup granulated sugar |
| 3 eggs, well beaten |
| 1/2 cup blanched almonds, finely chopped |
| 1/2 cup chopped mixed candied peel |
| finely grated peel of 1/2 lemon |
| juice and finely grated peel of 1/2 orange |
| 1/4 teaspoon vanilla extract |

**1** Sift the flour and salt into a mixing bowl and rub in the butter until the mixture resembles fine breadcrumbs. Mix in the egg yolk and enough iced water to form a soft dough. Knead lightly and leave to chill in the refrigerator for 30 minutes. Roll out the pastry to line an 8-inch quiche pan. Reserve the pastry trimmings.

**3** Pour the ricotta cheese filling into the prepared pastry shell and then smooth over the surface.

**4** Roll out the reserved pastry trimmings and then, using a fluted roller, cut into thin 1/2-inch wide strips. Arrange them in a criss-cross pattern over the top of the tart. Bake in

the center of a preheated oven at 350° for 45-50 minutes, or until set and golden. Cool and serve cold, rather than chilled, dusted with confectioners' sugar.

**2** Make the filling: rub the ricotta cheese through a sieve into a bowl and then beat in the sugar. Gradually beat in the eggs, and then add the almonds, peel, lemon and orange peel and juice and the vanilla, beating well between each addition.

PREPARATION: 20 MINUTES + 30 MINUTES CHILLING
COOKING: 45-50 MINUTES
SERVES: 6-8

# ARANCE GLASSATE
*Caramelized oranges*

12 oranges

³/₄ cup sugar

¹/₂ cup water

**1** Thinly pare the peel from one of the oranges and cut it into fine strips. Cook the strips in a small pan of boiling water for 2-3 minutes, or until softened. Drain well and put aside.

**2** Carefully remove all the pith and peel from the oranges with a sharp knife and put them in a large heatproof bowl. Sprinkle the strips of orange peel over the top.

**3** Put the sugar and water in a saucepan and heat gently, stirring constantly, until the sugar dissolves completely. Bring to the boil and boil hard until the syrup changes to a rich golden caramel. Take care that the caramel does not become too dark as it will continue to cook after the pan is removed from the heat.

**4** Pour the caramel over the oranges and set aside to cool. Put in the refrigerator and leave to chill overnight. To serve, transfer the oranges and caramel to an attractive serving dish and serve with whipped cream. Note: if wished, the oranges can be thinly sliced and secured with toothpicks before adding the caramel.

PREPARATION: 15 MINUTES
COOKING: 8-10 MINUTES +
CHILLING TIME
SERVES: 6-12

# SOUFFLE DI AMARETTO

*Amaretto almond soufflés*

4 macaroons

¹/₃ cup Amaretto di Saronno

²/₃ cup milk

1 drop of vanilla extract

1 tablespoon butter

¹/₄ cup all-purpose flour

4 egg yolks (1 kept separately)

4 egg whites

2 tablespoons granulated sugar

sifted confectioners' sugar to decorate

**For the almond purée:**

³/₄ cup slivered almonds

²/₃ cup milk

2 teaspoons sugar

**2** Grease and flour four 3-inch individual soufflé dishes. Soak the macaroons in half of the Amaretto and put one macaroon, cut into quarters, in each prepared soufflé dish.

**1** Make the almond purée: put the almonds, milk and sugar in a saucepan and bring to the boil. Reduce the heat and simmer gently for a few minutes. Cool slightly and then blend in a food processor or blender until thoroughly mixed.

PREPARATION: 25 MINUTES
COOKING: 10-12 MINUTES
SERVES: 4

**3** Make the soufflés: put two-thirds of the milk in a heavy saucepan with the vanilla and butter and bring to the boil. Remove from the heat and stir in the remaining milk with the flour and one egg yolk. Heat again until the mixture thickens and whisk briefly. Add the remaining egg yolks and cook for 2 minutes over low heat.

**4** Whisk the egg whites until stiff and then whisk in the sugar. Blend the soufflé mixture with the almond purée and remaining Amaretto. Carefully fold in the beaten egg whites. Spoon this mixture into the soufflé dishes and cook in a preheated oven at 425° for 10-12 minutes. Dust with confectioners' sugar.

# TIRAMISU
*Mascarpone coffee dessert*

**1** Mix the egg yolks and sugar together in a bowl, beating with a wooden spoon until they are creamy. Add the vanilla and fold in the mascarpone cheese. The mixture should be thick and creamy.

**3** Arrange some of the soaked ladyfingers in the base of a large attractive glass serving bowl or 4 individual serving dishes. Cover with a layer of the mascarpone mixture.

**2** Make the strong black coffee in a jug or cafetière, then mix with the Marsala and brandy in a bowl. Quickly dip the ladyfingers in the coffee mixture. They should absorb just enough liquid to flavor them without going soggy and falling apart.

PREPARATION: 20 MINUTES
CHILLING: 3-4 HOURS
SERVES: 6

| |
| --- |
| 2 egg yolks |
| 2 tablespoons granulated sugar |
| few drops of vanilla extract |
| 1 cup mascarpone cheese |
| 3/4 cup strong black coffee |
| 2 tablespoons Marsala |
| 1 tablespoon brandy |
| 5 ounces ladyfingers |
| 1 tablespoon cocoa powder |
| 2 tablespoons grated semisweet dark chocolate |

**4** Continue layering alternate layers of ladyfingers and mascarpone, finishing with a top layer of mascarpone. Sift the cocoa over the top and sprinkle with grated chocolate. Chill in the refrigerator for 3-4 hours or until set. The flavor improves if the tiramisu is left overnight.

# SAUCES, BREAD AND CROUTONS

## BOLOGNESE MEAT SAUCE

| |
|---|
| 4 tablespoons olive oil |
| 1 onion, finely chopped |
| 1 garlic clove, minced |
| 4 bacon slices, rind removed and chopped |
| 1 carrot, diced |
| 1 celery stick, diced |
| 1 pound ground beef |
| 1/4 pound chicken livers, chopped |
| 2/3 cup red wine |
| salt and freshly ground black pepper |
| 1/2 cup milk |
| pinch of ground nutmeg |
| 3 tablespoons tomato paste |
| 1 3/4 cups canned chopped tomatoes |

Heat the oil in a saucepan and add the onion, garlic, bacon, carrot and celery. Cook until tender and golden brown. Add the ground beef and chopped chicken livers, and continue cooking over medium heat, stirring occasionally, until evenly brown. Add the red wine and seasoning and bring to the boil. Reduce the heat slightly and cook over medium heat until most of the wine has evaporated. Add the milk and nutmeg and cook gently until absorbed by the meat. Stir in the tomato paste and chopped tomatoes, and simmer very gently for at least 1 hour until the sauce is reduced and richly colored. This quantity will serve 4 people.

## SALSA DI POMODORO

*Tomato sauce*

| |
|---|
| 2 tablespoons olive oil |
| 1 onion, finely chopped |
| 1 garlic clove, minced |
| 2 pounds tomatoes, skinned and chopped |
| salt and freshly ground black pepper |
| pinch of sugar |
| few basil leaves, chopped |

Heat the olive oil in a saucepan and add the onion and garlic. Fry gently until soft and golden. Add the tomatoes and cook gently for 10-15 minutes, until the sauce thickens and reduces. Season with salt and pepper and a pinch of sugar. Just before serving, stir in the chopped basil. Serve with meat, fish or pasta. This quantity will serve 4 people.

## SALSA PER INSALATA
*Salad dressing*

| |
|---|
| 6 tablespoons fruity green olive oil |
| 2 tablespoons lemon juice or vinegar |
| pinch of salt |
| 1 garlic clove, minced (optional) |
| 2 anchovy fillets, crushed (optional) |

Mix the olive oil with the lemon juice or vinegar and blend thoroughly. Add the salt and the garlic and anchovy fillets (if using). This quantity will serve 4 people.

**Variations:** add chopped fresh basil or parsley, chopped scallions or onion to vary the flavor.

## SALSA DI POMODORO CRUDA
*Fresh uncooked tomato sauce*

| |
|---|
| 1 pound tomatoes, skinned and chopped |
| 1 small onion, finely chopped |
| 1 garlic clove, minced |
| 1/4 cup olive oil |
| salt and freshly ground black pepper |
| 1 tablespoon chopped fresh basil |

Mix all the ingredients together in a bowl until thoroughly blended. Let the sauce stand for 1 hour, preferably at room temperature. Serve with pasta. This quantity will serve 4 people.

## MAIONESE
*Mayonnaise*

| |
|---|
| 2 egg yolks |
| 1/2 teaspoon salt |
| 1 cup olive oil |
| 1 teaspoon lemon juice |

Put the egg yolks in a bowl and beat well with a whisk or a hand-held electric whisk until they are pale and creamy. Beat in the salt and then start adding the olive oil, drop by drop. Continue beating all the time and, as the mayonnaise starts to thicken, add the oil in a thin but steady stream, still beating. Beat in the lemon juice last of all, and then check the seasoning, adding more salt if necessary. For success, all the ingredients and utensils should be at room temperature. This quantity will serve 4-6 people.

# BRUSCHETTA
## *Garlic bread*

| |
|---|
| 8 thick slices wholemeal or coarse white bread |
| 4 garlic cloves, peeled |
| 6 tablespoons fruity green olive oil |
| salt and freshly ground black pepper |

Toast the bread under a hot broiler until it is crisp and golden on both sides. Alternatively, bake it in the oven until crisp. Rub the garlic cloves over the bread and then pour the olive oil over the top. Sprinkle with a little salt and ground black pepper. Serves 4.

**Note:** Italian-style ciabatta bread, which is available in most supermarkets, is best for making bruschetta.

**Variation:** You can smear the bruschetta with the pulp of a cut tomato, and pop back under the broiler for 1-2 minutes.

# CROSTINI DI PANE
## *Bread croûtons*

| |
|---|
| 4 thick slices white bread |
| olive oil for shallow-frying |

Remove the crusts from the bread and cut it into large dice. Heat the olive oil to a depth of $^1/_2$ inch in a large skillet until it is sizzling hot. Add the bread and fry quickly, turning occasionally, until the dice are crisp and golden all over. Remove with a slotted spoon and drain on paper towels. Serve as a garnish for soup.

# SALSA BALSAMELLA
## *White sauce*

| |
|---|
| $^1/_4$ cup butter |
| $^1/_2$ cup flour |
| $2^1/_2$ cups milk |
| salt and pepper |
| freshly grated nutmeg |

Melt the butter in a saucepan over low heat and stir in the flour until the mixture forms a roux (paste). Cook, stirring constantly, for 2 minutes. Do not allow the roux to brown. Remove the saucepan from the heat and gradually beat in the milk, a little at a time, until all the milk has been incorporated and the sauce is smooth. Return to the heat and bring to the boil, stirring all the time. Reduce the heat immediately and cook over low heat for 10-15 minutes. Season with salt, pepper and nutmeg. Use the sauce in pasta dishes such as lasagne and cannelloni. This makes about $2^1/_2$ cups.

# SALSA VERDE
## *Green sauce*

| |
|---|
| 8 tablespoons olive oil |
| 1 tablespoon lemon juice |
| 2 tablespoons chopped fresh parsley |
| 2 tablespoons finely chopped capers |
| 1 garlic clove, minced |
| 4 anchovy fillets, mashed |
| salt and freshly ground black pepper |

Mix the olive oil and lemon juice together, and then stir in the remaining

ingredients to make a thick vinaigrette. Store in an airtight covered container in the refrigerator for up to 1 week. Serve with broiled fish. This quantity will serve 4 people.

# BAGNA CAUDA
## *Garlic and anchovy dip*

| |
|---|
| 2 ounces canned anchovies |
| $^1/_4$ cup butter |
| 4 tablespoons olive oil |
| 3 garlic cloves, minced |
| 4 tablespoons heavy cream (optional) |

| **To serve:** |
|---|
| raw vegetables, e.g. carrot and celery sticks, sliced sweet peppers and fennel bulbs |

Drain the anchovies and chop them finely. Heat the butter and oil in a small saucepan and add the garlic and anchovies. Simmer over low heat for 10 minutes. Remove from the heat and set aside to cool slightly. Stir in the cream (if using) and serve warm as a dip with crudités (raw vegetables). Ideally, the pot of bagna cauda should be placed in the center of the table on a warming tray or transferred to a fondue pot, and people dip in and help themselves. This quantity will serve 4 people.

# INDEX